Explaining Spiritual Warfare

Ed Roebert

Sovereign World

Sovereign World Ltd
PO Box 777
Tonbridge
Kent TN11 0ZS
England

Scripture quotations are from the Holy Bible, New International Version, © Copyright the International Bible Society, inclusive language version 1999; published by Hodder and Stoughton.

ISBN 1 85240 327 6

Cover design by Paul Welti
Typeset by CRB Associates, Reepham, Norfolk
Printed in the United States of America

Contents

1

Warfare against Satan

The Christian life has been likened to many things. The apostle Paul compared it to a race that is run (1 Corinthians 9:24), a letter that is written (2 Corinthians 3:1–3), a building that is under construction (1 Corinthians 3:10–17) and a wrestling match (2 Timothy 2:5). However, perhaps the most common metaphor he uses of the Christian life is warfare.

Paul said to Timothy:

Endure hardship with us like a good soldier of Christ Jesus. No one serving as a soldier gets involved in civilian affairs, but rather tries to please the commanding officer.

(2 Timothy 2:3–4)

This passage tells us that to fight in God's army is a serious business. We must endure hardship, and avoid entanglement in the affairs of this life. We are fighting a formidable enemy in the person of the devil and his demons.

Spiritual warfare demands all the resources we have in Christ, but it results in our inheriting the good things of the kingdom. Our aim is to please our commanding officer, Jesus.

One of the most important passages of Scripture on the subject of spiritual warfare is found in 2 Corinthians 10:3–5:

For though we live in the world, we do not wage war as the world does. The weapons we fight with are not the weapons of the world. On the contrary, they have divine power to demolish strongholds.

Although we live in the very real material world, we also have to engage with the spiritual world. The person who has lived all his life in the realm of the five senses tends to dismiss the existence of any other world, but that doesn't disprove its existence. If we are unaware of the attacks which may come from demonic sources, we can suffer the effects in our ordinary physical lives.

These verses tell us that the enemy has strongholds. These are like fortresses where the devil has established himself in our minds, our bodies or our attitudes and refuses to move. This is all too common, yet it is a tragedy when a Christian is held captive by Satan. Jesus can set us free! *Now!*

God has provided wonderfully powerful and effective weapons for this purpose. They include prayer, fasting, praise and worship, the complete armor of God, and the name of Jesus. There is also the sword of the Spirit – the word of God.

We have only two options in the Christian life. We can either live in the light of God's truth or live according to the lies of the devil. Jesus said:

> *If you hold to my teaching, you are really my disciples. Then you will know the truth, and the truth will set you free.*
>
> (John 8:32)

Many Christians only experience partial victory and release because they live in the twilight zone of partial truth. But the more truth we know and understand, the freer we become. This includes the use of spiritual gifts. Some people think that only one or two gifts are available to each person. Yet God is prepared to operate all of his gifts through all of his children (1 Corinthians 12:6).

Some people believe that they have been born to live in the "furnace of affliction" and feel helpless against the bombardment of the devil. Yet we have authority *"to overcome all the power of the enemy; nothing will harm you"* (Luke 10:19). The truth can set us free.

There is no doubt that the greatest battlefield in the world is in the area of our minds. Peter instructed the church to *"prepare your minds for action"* (1 Peter 1:13). We need to know God's truth so that we can live in his freedom.

If we have accepted the world's values, we may believe words like "All religions lead to God," or "There is no help for some people," or "I was born a homosexual – God made me to be that way and I can't change." Paul said in 2 Corinthians 10:5 that:

> *We demolish arguments and every pretension that sets itself up against the knowledge of God, and we take captive every thought to make it obedient to Christ.*

We do this with the sword of the Spirit.

Paul wrote:

> *. . . whatever is true, whatever is noble, whatever is right, whatever is pure, whatever is lovely, whatever is admirable – if anything is excellent or praiseworthy – think about such things."* (Philippians 4:8)

Our thoughts and imagination must be reprogrammed by the word of God. As we feast on what is good, we are strengthened for spiritual warfare.

2

Our authority in warfare

There is a world of difference between power and authority!
Power is strength, brute force, and ability. A strong man has
the power in his muscles to lift heavy weights.

Authority, on the other hand, is legal power, permission,
or the right to do something. A traffic officer has authority to
stop a huge vehicle.

In the New Testament, two Greek words are translated
as power and authority. *Dunamis,* from which we get our
English words "dynamite" and "dynamic," is the word
usually used to refer to power. *Exousia,* on the other hand,
means "authority."

Through the indwelling presence of the Lord Jesus and by
his Holy Spirit, we have been given both power and authority. The risen Christ told the apostles, *"you will receive power
when the Holy Spirit comes on you"* (Acts 1:8). He had already
said to them that he knew Satan of old and had dominion
over him:

> *"I saw Satan fall like lightning from heaven. I have given you*
> *authority to trample on snakes and scorpions and to overcome*
> *all the power of the enemy."*   (Luke 10:18–19)

God's authority is ultimate and universal. It was displayed
in creation, when God said, *"Let there be light"* – and there
was light! (Genesis 1:3). He has *"power to throw you into hell"*
(Luke 12:5) and authority to set *"times and dates"* of the
restoration of the kingdom (Acts 1:7).

The Father delegated this authority to his Son. Jesus said *"All authority on heaven and on earth has been given to me"* (Matthew 28:18). The writer of Hebrews 1:3 says that *"The Son is the radiance of God's glory and the exact representation of his being, sustaining all things through his powerful word."*

Jesus has been granted *"authority over all people"* (John 17:2) and is also *"the Head over every power and authority"* (Colossians 2:10). He showed that he had authority to forgive sins (Luke 5:24; Mark 2:10; Matthew 9:6), to execute judgment (John 5:27), and to *"give eternal life"* (John 17:2). In his days on earth he plainly stated that he had the authority to lay down his own life and *"authority to take it up again"* (John 10:18). What authority!

The moment we receive Jesus, and believe in his name, he gives us authority: *"the right to become children of God"* (John 1:12). We are rescued from the dominion [*exousia*, authority] of darkness and brought *"into the kingdom of the Son"* (Colossians 1:13). Paul testified that when the Lord Jesus appeared to him on the road to Damascus, he told Paul that he was sending him to open people's eyes and *"turn them from darkness to light, and from the power* [exousia] *of Satan to God"* (Acts 26:18).

Authority over our own wills

Praise God, we have been delivered from the authority of Satan's kingdom and we are now members of the kingdom of God. This does not mean that we have been turned into robots. We still have authority over our own wills in many areas of life.

God calls us to do things – pray, witness, give, love, exercise the gifts of the Spirit and manifest the fruit of the Spirit – but leaves it to our wills. We can be vital and active Christians who really count in the kingdom, or we can remain weak and mediocre. It's up to us. We can have whatever we will!

Admittedly, God works in us *"to will and to act according to his good purpose,"* but we are called to *"do everything without complaining or arguing"* (Philippians 2:13, 14). These verses say in effect that God works in us but we need to cooperate with his Holy Spirit. He wants us to line up our wills with his.

What kind of Christian you will be in three hours' time, three days' time, or three years' time depends both on God and on you. You have authority over your will.

God has also given to us:

Authority over our lifestyles and possessions

Acts 5 tells us how Ananias and Sapphira sold property and then gave the proceeds to the apostles. Because they lied about the amount that was realized for its sale, the consequences were catastrophic. Yet Peter said, *"Didn't it belong to you before it was sold? And after it was sold, wasn't the money at your disposal* [exousia]*?"*

In other words, when we become Christians, God doesn't take everything away from us. He doesn't need anything; he possesses all things. What he wants from us, and what we were born for, is relationship. He does not manipulate or dominate us in a human way.

We have authority over things that we rightfully own. Yet the level of our relationship with our Lord will determine our lifestyles and our attitudes towards possessions. If he has our hearts, he has everything we possess.

Nevertheless, God gives his children authority beyond our wildest dreams. As his disciples, Jesus has delegated to us:

Authority to cast out demons

Jesus gave the twelve disciples *"power and authority to drive out all demons"* (Luke 9:1). Each Christian possesses this authority, and we have the right to exercise it when we correctly discern that someone is demonized. After repentance and renunciation of any occult activity, we can rebuke demons in the name of Jesus and invite the Holy Spirit to take their place.

Authority over sickness and disease

Jesus also gave the Twelve authority *"to heal every disease and sickness"* (Matthew 10:1). Later he said that among the signs accompanying those who believe, is that in his name *"they will place their hands on sick people, and they will get well"* (Mark 16:18).

As individuals we have the right to exercise this authority in our own bodies, and as parents we can exercise it in our own families. We have also been commanded to do this on behalf of the sick wherever we find them. It's our job to pray: we just believe God's word and leave the results up to him.

A newly converted man was diagnosed with cancer throughout his body. The surgeons had operated, seen there was no hope and simply closed him up again, giving him only three months to live. When his pastor heard about it, he said, "If you are willing, we will stay with you and walk through this experience with you." Instead of the man lying on his bed, he got up, prayed and fought the cancer with the support of his church. Some time later he was pronounced cured. Together they had taken authority over sickness.

Authority over other ways the enemy would harm us

Jesus said to the seventy-two workers, *"I have given you authority to trample on snakes and scorpions and to overcome all the power of the enemy; nothing will harm you"* (Luke 10:19). He was not instructing us to deliberately seek out snakes and scorpions as a test. Rather he is saying that if the devil tries to hurt us in such ways, we have authority over these attacks.

Paul tells us in Ephesians 6:10–20 that we must protect ourselves against the enemy and *"put on the full armor of God."* Only in this way will we take our *"stand against the devil's schemes"* and *"extinguish all the flaming arrows of the evil one."* When we do, Satan is unable to harm us.

Increasing authority in life

In the parable of the money given to the ten servants (Luke 10:11–27), Jesus makes it clear that if we use what he gives us, he will give us more. If we fail to use what he has given, though, he will take away what he has already given. It is the same with any authority that has been delegated to us. The more we make good use of it, the more authority we will be given to exercise in future.

3

Body, soul and spirit

Many Christians are familiar with James 4:7 which tells us:

Resist the devil, and he will flee from you.

Yet few seem to know how to resist the devil and fewer still actually do so in their daily lives.

Some people believe that we should call on God to resist the enemy for us. But the Lord has delegated this authority to us, and he will not override this. Unless we resist the devil, the devil will go on unresisted!

We need to know how to go about spiritual warfare, and then we need to do it. Failure to do this could result in the devil pushing us into sin and getting us into all sorts of bondages and fear. It could end in the destruction of our families, relationships, finances, health, church and even country. It is a serious issue.

Success in spiritual warfare depends partly on understanding where the devil usually attacks. It helps if we can understand what makes a human being "tick."

Three dimensions

Just as God is a trinity of Father, Son and Spirit, so people are trinities consisting of spirit, soul and body. God created our bodies for us to live in, breathed into us spirit, and we became living souls (Genesis 2:7). This three-fold unity is clearly indicated in 1 Thessalonians 5:23:

> *May God himself, the God of peace, sanctify you through and through. May your whole spirit, soul and body be kept blameless at the coming of our Lord Jesus Christ.*

In our bodies we relate to the physical world through our five senses of touch, taste, smell, sight and hearing. Our souls are actually our personalities, including the intellect, emotions and will. Our spirits enable us to have two-way communication with God, who is himself Spirit. Most Christians need to develop greatly in this area.

The bad news is that Satan tries to attack us in all three of these areas: body, soul, and spirit. The good news is that we can have constant victory if we are prepared to engage in spiritual warfare!

Peter tells us that the devil prowls around looking for someone to devour, but that we should:

> *Resist him, standing firm in the faith, because you know that your brothers and sisters throughout the world are undergoing the same kind of suffering. And the God of all grace, who called you to his eternal glory in Christ, after you have suffered a little while, will himself restore you and make you strong, firm and steadfast. To him be the power for ever and ever.*   (1 Peter 5:9–11)

Satan's attacks on our bodies

Just as Satan oppressed people with sickness at the time when Christ was on the earth, so today he is constantly trying to attack our bodies. The gospel accounts tell us that many sicknesses are caused by demons, for instance the crippled woman (Luke 13:10), the blind and mute man (Matthew 12:22), and the deaf and mute boy who suffered convulsions (Mark 9:25).

Peter made this connection when he told Cornelius and his household:

how God anointed Jesus of Nazareth with the Holy Spirit and power, and how he went around doing good and healing all who were under the power of the devil, because God was with him.   (Acts 10:38)

The devil is clearly responsible for sickness, but when he hits our bodies we can win out through spiritual warfare.

Satan's attacks on our souls

It is clear that the devil attacks us in all areas of our souls. In the Garden of Eden, the serpent placed a doubt in Eve's mind. So too, he attacks our intellects, often trying to implant doubts or false doctrines. For this reason we need to be firmly grounded in the word of God.

The devil also attacks our emotions, particularly when our minds have already been weakened. One of his most effective weapons is a spirit of fear: once we have received that, we are vulnerable to many other oppressive feelings. As mature Christians we should be able to identify these things and deal with them before they do damage.

Our wills can also be damaged by the devil. As a result we can become lazy, apathetic and sluggish, losing all motivation to live, to work and to achieve. We should be spiritually alert and take action as soon as we detect these symptoms, to avoid becoming unproductive.

Satan's attacks on our spirits

Some believe that our spirits are inaccessible to Satan and thus cannot be defiled, but the Bible says:

Since we have these promises, dear friends, let us purify ourselves from everything that contaminates body and spirit, perfecting holiness out of reverence for God.
(2 Corinthians 7:1)

Our conscience is our capacity to tell right from wrong. Paul says in his letter to Titus:

"To the pure, all things are pure, but to those who are corrupted and do not believe, both their minds and their consciences are corrupted."   (Titus 1:15)

We must keep the enemy from infiltrating our consciences in any way and take notice whenever they sound a warning bell.

We were created to communicate with God and to hear his voice. Often we can recognize things intuitively, that is, with our spirits. These channels must be kept clear of any occult influence so that we are guided only by the Holy Spirit. An ever-increasing knowledge of God's revealed word purifies our capacity to hear his voice and recognize true from false.

It is not always easy to distinguish between God's voice and that of the enemy. If it contradicts Scripture, we must reject it and take authority in the spiritual realms. As we consistently do this we will hear the voice of God more and more clearly. It will lead us into greater fruitfulness in every area of our lives.

4

Winning the war at home

The family unit is of great importance to God. God is a Father – he has created us in his image, as sons and daughters. Paul wrote,

> *I kneel before the Father, from whom his whole family in heaven and on earth derives its name.* (Ephesians 3:25)

He has built into us a longing for family life and is pleased to place us into families. The Bible gives considerable attention to the family and states clear guidelines as to how it should operate.

We know that the devil comes *"to steal and kill and destroy"* (John 10:10) anything that God has created. He is bent on the destruction of the family. Yet we have authority to stop him!

In Ephesians chapters 5 and 6, Paul gives godly advice to wives, husbands, children and fathers. The family that applies the principles of God's word is able to withstand the attacks of the enemy, but those who do not, leave themselves vulnerable. It is interesting that almost immediately following Paul's words in Ephesians about the family is a complete shift to instruction on spiritual warfare.

There is evidence that Satan's favorite target of spiritual warfare is the Christian family. None of us are immune to such attacks, but spiritually alert families can know consistent victory.

*Finally, be strong in the Lord and in his mighty power. Put on
the full armor of God so that you can take your stand against
the devil's schemes.*   (Ephesians 6:10–11)

Satan tries to destroy the divine order in the home

One of the three basic tactics that the devil uses against
Christian families is to destroy the order that God has
ordained. There is a God-given order in creation, in the
church, and in the home. If we submit ourselves to God
and line up our family lives with his will, then he takes
responsibility for our families.

In Genesis 1:26 we read that God said:

> *"Let us make human beings in our image, in our likeness, and
> let them rule ... over all the earth."*

He was calling the first families to govern the world! History
tells us that entire nations have collapsed when they have
ignored the basic structure of the family.

The enemy's very first attack on human beings successfully
disrupted the divine order of family life. He tricked Eve into
assuming leadership of the family, while Adam abdicated his
role as protector. This tragic reversal of roles led to rebellion,
disobedience, and broken fellowship with God.

Husbands must ask themselves, "Am I abdicating my God-
given role as head of the family? Am I failing to fulfill my
responsibilities or exercise godly authority?" Wives must ask
themselves, "Do I manipulate or dominate my husband? Am
I frequently critical of his leadership?" There can be demonic
spirits behind these behaviors. If the answer to these ques-
tions is yes, then confession and repentance are needed.

Such marriage problems are often passed down from
generation to generation. To break out of these patterns it is
necessary to cut any ungodly ties with past generations. We
can pray in faith to break these curses while still retaining the
good and healthy aspects of our family heritage.

Satan tries to bring occult influences into the home

The forms of the occult that we may now encounter in our daily lives are countless. It is little wonder that individuals and families struggle to keep themselves clear of such influences.

One way that we encounter the occult is through the media. Thousands of magazines and newspapers regularly print horoscopes. Many television programs focus on the occult in various ways.

We also encounter the occult through medical or quasi-medical practitioners. Acupuncture, reflexology, homeopathy, iridology, use of pendulums, certain herbal remedies with a link to witchcraft, and hypnosis are all ways of seeking healing that can be dangerous.

A general fascination with magic can open both adults and children to occult influences. Activities such as experimenting with a glass on the table or Ouija boards, mesmerism, automatic writing, crystal gazing, using charms, fortune telling through palm-reading or tea leaves, as well as attending séances are all in this category. Through Halloween festivities and children's stories, witches and sorcerers may now have a reputation as fun and harmless, which is very misleading.

There is also an occult influence in some sports. Yoga and martial arts such as karate may appear innocent but have origins in Eastern religions. The serious follower can be involved in meditations and even incantations as well as philosophy contrary to Christian teaching.

The Bible forbids any occult involvement (Deuteronomy 18:9–14). We should *"Test everything. Hold onto the good. Avoid any kind of evil"* (1 Thessalonians 5:21–22). Don't give the devil a foothold!

Satan tries to destroy the family through lies and accusations

The devil is well-named the "slanderer" and "the accuser." He is an expert at such things. Jesus said,

"He was a murderer from the beginning, not holding to the truth, for there is no truth in him. When he lies, he speaks his native language, for he is a liar and the father of lies."
(John 8:44)

The devil's accusations can fan our fears into discouragement and despair.

One common area of attack is the husband–wife relationship. At times of stress, the devil whispers lies such as "Your marriage will never change." "Your partner doesn't really love you." "Get divorced – you could do much better." Many people battle with financial issues and the devil can encourage us to doubt God's provision in this area. Yet persistent faith in God's promises will be rewarded.

Those who are single may also struggle with relationships, especially if they have experienced bereavement or divorce. Feelings of loneliness and rejection can come to the surface for those who live on their own. Some feel of less value than those who have found a life partner, and the enemy capitalizes on that.

Raising children is not the easiest of responsibilities. Anger and bitterness can erupt even in Christian families. In parent–child relationships, we can hear such lies as "You've failed as parents!" or "Your children will never amount to much." The devil's aim is to paralyze us with fear, torment us with suspicion, provoke us to wrath or drive us to despair. It helps greatly if we can recognize who the attacker is and resist him with determination.

Health is another area of struggle for many. We may believe lies from Satan such as "Your grandfather died of a heart attack at forty – you're going the same way" or "That headache must be a tumor." It's easy to assume that we should expect a spate of colds and viruses all winter and whenever there is a change of weather. But we can take authority by remembering that God has built into our bodies healing capabilities. Expect to get better, and ask Jesus for healing in his name.

There are five steps to victory!

1. **Get angry with the devil.** Don't sit and take it any longer. Remind yourself that Satan is a liar, a thief, a destroyer and a murderer.
2. **Understand that you have authority over the devil.** God gave it to you to exercise!
3. **Resist the devil when he attacks.** Speak out against him!
4. **Keep short accounts.** Don't let sin into your life.
5. **Make praise a lifestyle.** Develop a positive attitude of praising God in all situations.

5

The spirit of this age

Christian growth towards maturity doesn't take place automatically. We have to take decisive steps to progress. Part of this is making sure that we are not caught up in *"the present evil age"* (Galatians 1:4).

When people responded to the preaching of Peter on the day of Pentecost, he pleaded with them to *"save yourselves from this corrupt generation"* (Acts 2:40). The Greek word for "corrupt" is *skolias*, as in the word "scoliosis" that describes the curvature of the spine. It is also translated "crooked"; this passage is saying that we are not to get warped, twisted, or bent out of God's shape for us.

We need to preserve ourselves from the perverse spirit of this age. We must deliver ourselves from the influences, opinions, and ultimate fate of the unredeemed people around us, through repentance and baptism in the name of Jesus.

It is obvious that evil influences and spirits were at work when Peter spoke those words, and such influences have continued to operate ever since. Paul, writing to Timothy, made it clear that this would increasingly be the case as the end draws near:

> *But mark this: There will be terrible times in the last days. People will be lovers of themselves, lovers of money, boastful, proud, abusive, disobedient to their parents, ungrateful, unholy, without love, unforgiving, slanderous, without self-control, brutal, not lovers of the good, treacherous, rash,*

> *conceited, lovers of pleasure rather than lovers of God –*
> *having a form of godliness but denying its power. Have*
> *nothing to do with them.*   (2 Timothy 3:1–5)

There are three sources of temptation that we need to deal
with: the world, the flesh and the devil.

The world – and its materialism

John wrote to the early church:

> *Do not love the world or anything in the world ... For*
> *everything in the world – the cravings of sinful people, the*
> *lust of their eyes and the boasting of what they have and do –*
> *comes not from the Father but from the world.*
>   (1 John 2:15, 16)

The Greek word *kosmos*, translated "the world" or "this age,"
refers to the present world system. It is controlled by a spirit
other than the Holy Spirit of God (1 Corinthians 2:12). Paul
speaks of Satan as *"The god of this age [who] has blinded the*
minds of unbelievers" (2 Corinthians 4:4). John says that *"the*
whole world is under the control of the evil one" (1 John 5:19).

Many people are totally trapped by the materialistic spirit
of this age. In pursuit of money and material possessions,
some have lost their families, health and happiness. Yet it's
like a sickness. The money-mad person is never satisfied,
however many millions he acquires.

John warns us to beware of the lust of the eyes: that is,
desiring everything our eyes see! Particularly in our present
culture, the advertising world aggressively offers us so much
that we don't really need.

Jesus said:

> *"No one can be a slave to two masters. Either you will hate*
> *the one and love the other, or you will be devoted to the one*
> *and despise the other. You cannot be a slave to both God and*
> *money."*   (Matthew 6:24)

Devotion to money is directly opposed to devotion to God. Paul adds:

> For the love of money is a root of all kinds of evil. Some people, eager for money, have wandered from the faith and pierced themselves with many griefs ... Command those who are rich in this present world not to be arrogant nor to put their hope in wealth, which is so uncertain, but to put their hope in God, who richly provides us with everything for our enjoyment. Command them to do good, to be rich in good deeds, and to be generous and willing to share.
>
> (1 Timothy 6:10, 17–18)

This worldly system will not last forever. It will be defeated!

> "Now is the time for judgment on this world; now the prince of this world will be driven out." (John 12:31)

> "... the prince of this world now stands condemned." (John 16:11)

> The world and its desires pass away, but whoever does the will of God lives forever. (1 John 2:17)

We Christians have been translated out of this worldly system into the kingdom of Jesus.

> For he has rescued us from the dominion of darkness and brought us into the kingdom of the Son he loves.
>
> (Colossians 1:13)

This is why John tells us not to love the present world (1 John 2:15), even though its pull is considerable. Not only are we attracted by the things of the world but we are greatly influenced by its philosophies, stated and unstated. We must resist this attraction and *"set your hearts on things above, not on earthly things"* (Colossians 3:2).

It is a question of having our priorities right. Jesus said, after telling us not to run after the things of the world as the pagans do, that we should *"seek first his kingdom and his righteousness, and all these things will be given to you as well"*

(Matthew 6:33). If we place things first, the Lord cannot be first, but if we place the Lord first then he will give us all the things we need.

It is vital that we are not swept off our feet by worldly things and ideas. Although we cannot take ourselves out of the world, we can stoutly resist ungodly influences in our lives. We are in the world but not of it.

The flesh – and its lusts

The word "flesh" is used to refer to the physical body and also to sinful human nature. Some philosophers have believed that the human body is essentially evil, but this is not so. Our human flesh is neutral, neither intrinsically sinful nor holy.

However, this worldly system is corrupted by lust and other evil desires. We read in 2 Peter 1:4 that Jesus enables us to participate in the divine nature so that we can *"escape the corruption of the world caused by evil desires."*

Paul lists many "works of the flesh" that Christians must turn away from:

> *The acts of the sinful nature are obvious: sexual immorality, impurity and debauchery; idolatry and witchcraft; hatred, discord, jealousy, fits of rage, selfish ambition, dissensions, factions and envy; drunkenness, orgies and the like. I warn you, as I did before that those who live like this will not inherit the kingdom of God.*   (Galatians 5:19–21)

This list includes moral sins (sexual immorality, impurity and debauchery), spiritual sins (idolatry and witchcraft) and social sins (hatred, discord, jealousy, fits of rage, etc.) They are all incompatible with the kingdom of God.

The flesh is in direct opposition to the Holy Spirit.

> *For the sinful nature desires what is contrary to the Spirit, and the Spirit what is contrary to the sinful nature. They are in conflict with each other, so that you do not do what you want.*
> (Galatians 5:17)

Living under the influence of the sinful nature brings spiritual death:

> *The mind controlled by the sinful nature is death ... the sinful mind is hostile to God. It does not submit to God's law, nor can it do so. Those controlled by the sinful nature cannot please God ... For if you live according to the sinful nature, you will die.*   (Romans 8:6–8, 13)

> *Therefore, brothers and sisters, we have an obligation – but it is not to the sinful nature, to live according to it.*
> (Romans 8:12)

We owe the flesh nothing! We counteract its influences by recognizing what is of the sinful nature, resisting and rejecting it by spiritual warfare, and by living in the Spirit. We overcome the sinful nature by obeying the Holy Spirit:

> *So I say, live by the Spirit, and you will not gratify the desires of the sinful nature.*   (Galatians 5:16)

> *If by the Spirit you put to death the misdeeds of the body, you will live, because those who are led by the Spirit of God are children of God.*   (Romans 8:13–14)

One of the areas most damaging to our spiritual life is sexual immorality. Through the influence of the media, pre-marital sex and adultery (sex that breaks the marriage bond), homosexuality and other forms of perversion have become generally accepted in our society. This has led to the erosion of the family and left many open to demonic influences.

There is a better way! We can repent of and confess our sins, and learn to walk in the Spirit.

> *Live by the Spirit, and you will not gratify the desires of the sinful nature.*   (Galatians 5:16)

The devil – and the occult

The basic meaning of the word occult is "secret or hidden."

This pertains to the knowledge of forbidden areas of the supernatural. The spectrum of false religious ideas includes the New Age movement, ESP, Rosicrucianism, spiritism, witchcraft, Unity "School of Truth", Swedenborgianism, Christadelphianism, Mormonism, Baha'i, Scientology, theosophy, Science of Mind, and many others.

Most forms of the occult contain three fundamental ideas:

1.   God is in everything; everything is God; therefore we ourselves are gods.

2.   The devil is not a person or a reality.

3.   There is no sin, no need for atonement through the blood of Jesus, no repentance, and no Savior.

Deuteronomy 18:9–14 provides a stern warning against occult involvement:

> *When you enter the land the LORD your God is giving you, do not learn to imitate the detestable ways of the nations there. Let no one be found among you who sacrifices a son or daughter in the fire, who practices divination or sorcery, interprets omens, engages in witchcraft or casts spells, or who is a medium or spiritist or who consults the dead. Anyone who does these things is detestable to the LORD ... The nations you will dispossess listen to those who practice sorcery or divination. But as for you, the LORD your God has not permitted you to do so.*

Note also the following references: 2 Kings 17:17, 18; 21:1–6; and 23:24 (describing the disobedience of kings of Israel in following occult ways, incurring God's anger); 1 Chronicles 10:13, 14 and 1 Samuel 28:5–20 (about Saul's unfaithfulness to the Lord, consulting a medium instead of asking God for guidance); and Isaiah 2:6, 8, 18; 47:13 (prophecies against astrologers and the worship of idols).

The current flood-tide of the occult was prophesied in 1 Timothy 4:1:

The Spirit clearly says that in later times some will abandon the faith and follow deceiving spirits and things taught by demons.

We can be released from these things by confessing all occult involvement as sin, and by destroying all books, objects and related materials as the new believers did in Acts 19:18–19. After coming clean, we can stay clean by completely yielding ourselves to God and resisting the devil.

We can do this with a statement such as:

Satan, in the name of the Lord Jesus Christ I reject you and the influences you have exercised over my life. Through the blood of Jesus I am cleansed from all sin and involvement in the occult. Jesus Christ alone is my Lord.

I completely break any tie I may ever have had with you, Satan, and tell you to get out of my life forever. I refuse and resist any evil force that would seek to influence me. I break all bondages in the name of Jesus Christ and in the power of his blood.

That settles it! Be filled with the Spirit, be obedient to God, and continue to stand firm in your faith.

6

Satan and his evil spirits

Evil spirits are fallen angels (2 Peter 2:4). They are also called
"powers of this dark world" and *"spiritual forces of evil in the
heavenly realm"* (Ephesians 6:12), demons and *"deceiving
spirits"* (1 Timothy 4:1).

Satan, the leader of the evil spirits, seems at one time to
have outranked even Michael and Gabriel, the leaders of the
angelic hosts. However, because of his pride he became
the source of all the anarchy and rebellion in the world.
Many either deny him or see him merely as an impersonal
evil force. But the Bible depicts him personally:

> *Your enemy the devil prowls around like a roaring lion looking*
> *for someone to devour.* (1 Peter 5:8)

In 2 Corinthians 4:4 Satan is described as *"the god of this
age"* and in Ephesians 2:2 he is described as *"the ruler of the
kingdom of the air, the spirit who is now at work in those who are
disobedient."* He is also called the devil, Beelzebub, Belial, the
adversary, dragon and serpent. By one or other of these
names he is mentioned 174 times in the Bible.

Satan's origin is somewhat shrouded in mystery. Yet
Ezekiel and Isaiah together paint a picture for us:

> *You were the model of perfection,*
> *full of wisdom and perfect in beauty.*

You were in Eden,
the garden of God;
every precious stone adorned you . . .
You were anointed as a guardian cherub,
for so I ordained you.
You were on the holy mount of God;
you walked among the fiery stones.
You were blameless in your ways
from the day you were created
until wickedness was found in you. (Ezekiel 28:12–15)

We see that he was a created being; he was exceptionally beautiful and wise; he was anointed as a guardian (so possibly head of the angelic hierarchy); and went from blamelessness to wickedness. The passage goes on to describe his fall:

Through your widespread trade
you were filled with violence,
and you sinned.
So I drove you in disgrace from the mount of God,
and I expelled you, O guardian cherub,
from among the fiery stones.
Your heart became proud
on account of your beauty,
and you corrupted your wisdom
because of your splendor.
So I threw you to the earth . . . (Ezekiel 28:16, 17)

Because of his sin, Satan was driven out of heaven. His ultimate destruction – *"a horrible end"* is also foretold in the successive verses.

Isaiah adds more detail to the picture:

How you have fallen from heaven,
O morning star, son of the dawn!
You have been cast down to the earth,
you who once laid low the nations!
You said in your heart,
"I will ascend to heaven;

I will raise my throne
  above the stars of God;
I will sit enthroned on the mount of assembly,
  on the utmost heights of the sacred mountain.
I will ascend above the tops of the clouds;
  I will make myself like the Most High."

(Isaiah 14:12–14)

Satan's presumption and pride is evident here – he sought to rival God. Isaiah also speaks of his final downfall:

But you are brought down to the grave,
  to the depths of the pit. (Isaiah 14:15)

At present he is not only ruling the air, but *"roaming through the earth and going to and fro in it"* (Job 1:7). Jesus had an encounter with the devil in the wilderness (Matthew 4:1–11).

Jesus makes it clear that Satan is a king with a kingdom (Matthew 12:26). His kingdom is governed by a hierarchy, which we understand from Ephesians 6:12:

> *Our struggle is not against flesh and blood, but against the rulers, against the authorities, against the powers of this dark world and against the spiritual forces of evil in the heavenly realms.*

Daniel 10:13 and 21 suggest that he has princes ruling over different countries.

It is evident that Satan works to deceive both nations (Revelation 20:3) and individuals. Matthew 24:24 tells us that he sends out false prophets and false messiahs, *"to deceive even the elect – if that were possible."* He also tries to bring condemnation and guilt on us: Revelation 12:10 calls him *"the accuser of our brothers and sisters, who accuses them before our God day and night."*

However, Jesus came to defeat Satan.

> *The reason the Son of God appeared was to destroy the devil's work.* (1 John 3:8)

As Christians today, we also have this authority over Satan. James 4:7 tells us:

> *Resist the devil, and he will flee from you.*

And we know that ultimately, his doom is settled! (Revelation 12:9–12; 20:1–3, 10).

7

Manifestations of evil spirits

The Bible compares the Christian life to warfare between the forces of darkness and the forces of light. Paul says:

> *The weapons we fight with are not the weapons of the world. On the contrary, they have divine power to demolish strongholds.* (2 Corinthians 10:4)

In this war we use spiritual weapons to fight against invisible forces. Because we are unable to see the devil and his demons with our physical eyes, we need to be able to discern their presence.

We read in the Bible of good spirits that come from God. These include the *"Spirit of truth"* (1 John 4:6), the *"spirit of faith"* (2 Corinthians 4:13), the *"Spirit of wisdom and revelation"* (Ephesians 1:17) and the *"Spirit of glory"* (1 Peter 4:14). In fact, these are all manifestations of the Holy Spirit.

Then there are the evil spirits that originate from the devil, sometimes called *"unclean spirits,"* a general term that covers all forms of demonic manifestation. We can identify them through the gift of discernment of spirits. We can also observe their manifestations – the usual ways in which they operate and the carnage they leave behind them.

There are unholy spirits that can oppress or possess us. Romans 8:15 speaks of a *"spirit that makes you a slave to fear."* Any spirit that enslaves us is from the devil. We can be slaves to all sorts of sin such as lust, greed, and addictions to cigarettes, alcohol, drugs, gambling, etc. Paul speaks of a *"spirit of timidity"* in 2 Timothy 1:7, and such a spirit may prevent believers from stepping out in faith to do the work God has called them to.

Many people are affected by ungodly fears, including the *"fear of death"* (Hebrews 2:14–15) and the fear of people's opinions (Proverbs 29:25). Such fears manifest themselves in nightmares, stress, agitation, worry, terror, foreboding and dread. They can result in physical conditions of many sorts including ulcers, heart attacks and nervous conditions such as claustrophobia and agoraphobia. Some people become recluses because of such fears, while others turn to obsessive perfectionism.

Jealousy can be linked to unholy spirits: the first murder was linked to jealousy, anger and the desire for revenge (Genesis 4). Joseph's brothers tried to destroy him because of their jealousy and hatred (Genesis 37). In Galatians 5:20 and 21, Paul links jealousy with hatred, discord, fits of rage, selfish ambition, dissensions, factions, and envy as part of the *"acts of the sinful nature."* None of them are compatible with the Holy Spirit.

Isaiah says that the Spirit of the Lord is sent that we may have *"a crown of beauty instead of ashes, the oil of gladness instead of mourning, and a garment of praise instead of a spirit of despair"* (Isaiah 61:3). Many people are afflicted by a spirit of despair: depression, a constant sense of heaviness, hopelessness, and discouragement, sometimes to the point of suicide. This spirit often takes advantage of a weakened physical condition and emotional state; discernment is needed!

In Romans 11:8, Paul quotes Deuteronomy 29:4 and Isaiah 29:10 in regard to unbelieving Jews:

> *God gave them a spirit of stupor,*
> *eyes so that they could not see*
> *and ears so that they could not hear.*

This spirit of apathy, sluggishness and idleness makes people deaf and blind to the truth of God, and is the opposite of the spirit of *"wisdom and revelation"* spoken of in Ephesians.

John speaks of *"the spirit of falsehood"* (1 John 4:6), which causes people to be unteachable and to promote erroneous doctrines. A spirit of falsehood may be linked with a critical and unloving spirit which is why John goes on to teach on the subject of love in the successive verses. He also mentions the *"spirit of the antichrist"* which does not acknowledge the incarnation of Jesus. Paul also speaks of *"deceiving spirits"* (1 Timothy 4:1) that try to lead believers astray.

In 1 Kings 22:21–23 a *"lying spirit"* appears. Some people tell lies or swear compulsively, and others speak maliciously about fellow Christians. A lying spirit may lead people to take up superstitious practices or to follow false religions.

Any spirit that opposes Christ or attempts to take the place of Christ is demonic. We should be alert to any effort to refute Jesus' deity and humanity or his death on the cross. Spirits of legalism will place heavy demands on people and try to bind them to laws that are not required by Scripture. Someone who tries to disturb church meetings, attack Christians or blaspheme the gifts of the Holy Spirit may be influenced by a spirit of falsehood or the antichrist.

Proverbs 16:18 says that

> *Pride goes before destruction,*
> *a haughty spirit before a fall.*

A haughty, proud spirit has been the downfall of many, including the devil himself. Egotism, self-righteousness, arrogance, insolence, and a controlling and domineering spirit can be linked to this. Peter quotes Proverbs 3:34:

> *God opposes the proud but gives grace to the humble.*
> (1 Peter 5:5)

Hosea spoke against a *"spirit of prostitution"* leading the people of Israel astray. This can include any kind of idolatry or unfaithfulness to God. It can also be linked to sexual immorality, as is described in Romans 1:18–32. The message is that because people turned to idols *"God gave them over . . . to sexual impurity for the degrading of their bodies."* The worship of Baal and Asherah, for instance by Ahab and Jezebel (1 Kings 16–22; 2 Kings 9–10), combines idolatry and sexual sin.

Jesus often dealt with evil spirits in his earthly ministry. The man possessed by a *"legion of demons"* (Mark 5:1–17) had supernatural strength so that he could not even be bound by chains, and wandered around in isolated places, crying out and cutting himself with stones. After his deliverance, he was *"dressed and in his right mind,"* implying that he had previously been known as naked and insane.

The account of the boy with the deaf and mute spirit (Mark 9:14–29), says that this spirit, which *"robbed him of speech,"* threw the boy to the ground in convulsions, so that he foamed at the mouth, gnashed his teeth and became rigid. The boy's father said: *"It has often thrown him into fire or water to kill him"* as if the demon's intent was to cause him to commit suicide. It is clear that the disciples had difficulty casting out this spirit (see also Matthew 17:14–18). Notice also that when Jesus healed the boy he first lay on the ground as though dead. In Luke's account the father says that the boy *"suddenly screams"* when the *"spirit seizes him,"* that it *"scarcely ever leaves him and is destroying him"* (Luke 9:27–42).

Matthew (12:22) tells the story of Jesus healing a *"demon-possessed man who was blind and mute,"* indicating that demons can also cause blindness. In Luke 13:10–16, we read the story of a woman who had been *"crippled by a spirit for eighteen years"*; she was bent over so that she could not straighten up at all. Jesus calls it an *"infirmity,"* which could be applied to all kinds of frailty, disease, and weakness.

In Luke 4:33–36, a man possessed by a demon challenged Jesus in the synagogue. The man *"cried out at the top of his voice"* while trying to taunt Jesus with his knowledge of Jesus as the holy one of God. Similarly, the man with the legion of demons came out of the tombs to find Jesus as if compelled to meet him.

The early church had to confront a spirit of divination (Acts 16:16–18). Luke says that they met *"a female slave who had a spirit by which she predicted the future"* – literally, "the spirit of a python." People who are involved in fortune telling, water divining, clairvoyance, consulting with the dead or with familiar spirits (spirit guides), and other occult activities need deliverance just as the slave woman did.

Knowledge of demonic manifestations can assist us in our warfare against spiritual powers. As we recognize the devil's wiles we are more able to uncover, resist and cast out evil spirits. But unless we actually act on the knowledge we have, we will not be able to live in victory and blessing.

8

The ministry of angels

The Bible clearly teaches that there are unfallen angels able to minister to us and assist us in spiritual warfare.

There are *"thousands upon thousands of angels"* (Hebrews 12:22). They are referred to as *"powerful"* (2 Thessalonians 1:7) although they are not all-powerful. They are glorious beings, according to Luke 9:26, and they seem to possess great knowledge although they are not omniscient (all-knowing).

The angels are all *"ministering spirits sent to serve those who will inherit salvation"* (Hebrews 1:14). It was an angel that rolled away the heavy stone from the tomb of Jesus. They are also responsible for punishing *"those who do not know God and do not obey the gospel of our Lord Jesus"* (2 Thessalonians 1:8). A single angel destroyed 185,000 of the Assyrian army in a night (2 Kings 19:35) and one day an angel will bind Satan and cast him into the bottomless pit.

Among the angels there are two significant leaders.

▶ **Archangel Michael** is mentioned three times in the book of Daniel, where he is described as *"the great prince who protects your people"* (Daniel 12:1). In Revelation 12:7 he is pictured commanding the army of heaven. Jude 9 speaks of him rebuking the devil in connection with Moses' body, and 1 Thessalonians 4:16 says that the *"voice of the archangel"* will accompany the Lord's return and the resurrection of the dead.

43

► **Gabriel** explained the meaning of a vision to Daniel (Daniel 8:16). Later he came again to Daniel and spoke of the coming of the anointed one, Christ (Daniel 9:21–27). Fittingly, Gabriel announced John the Baptist's birth and also told Mary that she was to give birth to Jesus (Luke 1:11–20; 26–38). When Zechariah doubted his words, he rebuked him, saying *"I am Gabriel. I stand in the presence of God,"* indicating his significant position in heaven.

Angels and the life and ministry of Jesus

After Gabriel prophesied Jesus' conception and birth to Mary, an angel appeared to Joseph to confirm that the pregnancy was a direct act of the Holy Spirit (Matthew 1:18–23).

An angel of the Lord appeared to the shepherds to announce the news of Jesus' birth, and *"a great company of the heavenly host"* appeared, praising God (Luke 2:9–15). Angels protected Jesus as an infant, warning his parents to flee to Egypt (Matthew 2:13–15). Later, an angel directed Joseph to return to the land of Israel after Herod's death (Matthew 2:19–21).

After Jesus' temptation in the wilderness, angels *"came and attended him"* (Matthew 4:11). As he was in anguish at Gethsemane, *"An angel from heaven appeared to him and strengthened him"* (Luke 22:43). Rebuking the disciple who attacked the high priest's servant with his sword, Jesus asked, *"Do you think I cannot call on my Father, and he will at once put at my disposal more than twelve legions of angels?"* (Matthew 26:53).

At the resurrection,

> *There was a violent earthquake, for an angel of the Lord came down from heaven and, going to the tomb, rolled back the stone and sat on it. His appearance was like lightning, and his clothes were white as snow. The guards were so afraid of him that they shook and became like dead men.*
>
> (Matthew 28:2–4)

Two angels appeared to the women who went to the tomb, described as *"two men in clothes that gleamed like lightning,"* and announced that Jesus had risen (Luke 24:4–6).

Luke records that at the ascension, *"two men dressed in white"* stood beside the disciples and prophesied Jesus' second coming (Acts 1:11). Matthew says that the Son of Man (Jesus) *"will send his angels with a loud trumpet call"* to gather the elect (Matthew 24:31), and that all the angels will accompany him as he comes in glory.

Peter wrote that *"even angels long to look"* into the mysteries of salvation (1 Peter 1:12) and that they, along with authorities and powers are in submission to Christ (1 Peter 3:22). The letter to the Hebrews quotes an ancient Scripture passage, *"Let all God's angels worship him"* (Hebrews 1:6).

How angels help us

▶ Angels assist us by doing spiritual warfare against devilish powers

This is the clear teaching of Daniel 10. While seeking God in a fast, he saw an amazing vision which caused him to fall with his face to the ground. The dazzling person in his vision said that he had come in response to Daniel's prayers, but been delayed for 31 days by *"the prince of the Persian kingdom,"* a spiritual authority controlling the dominion of Persia.

The man told Daniel that Michael (possibly the archangel of Jude 9), *"one of the chief princes"* had come to help him. It is evident that the angels assist each other in their spiritual warfare! As a result, a breakthrough happened and the man came to tell the meaning of an important vision to Daniel.

▶ Angels bring revelation to the saints

This is clear from many of the passages about the life of Jesus. Indeed, it was an angel who made the revelation of the end times known to John (Revelation 1:1).

► **Angels provide guidance**

They seem to be particularly concerned with salvation, and guided the disciples as they spread the gospel. An angel directed Philip down the desert road so that he could meet the Ethiopian official and explain the good news of Jesus to him (Acts 8:26). An angel told Cornelius to send for Peter who would inform him how to be saved (Acts 10:1–8; 11:13, 14).

► **Angels also participate in God's encouragement and provision**

An angel encouraged Hagar and directed her and her son to water (Genesis 21:17–20). The manna provided for the wandering Israelites was called *"the bread of angels"* (Psalm 78:25). Just before Paul was shipwrecked, an angel brought words of encouragement for him and the other sailors (Acts 27). We read in Daniel 10:18, 19 that

> *Again the one who looked like a man touched me and gave me strength. "Do not be afraid, O man highly esteemed", he said. "Peace! Be strong now, be strong." When he spoke to me, I was strengthened ...*

The angels can strengthen us, encourage us, and speak words of peace and revelation from God himself.

► **Angels are active in protecting and delivering God's people**

When Daniel was thrown into the lion's den, an angel shut the lions' mouths (Daniel 6:20–23). An angel of the Lord *"opened the doors of the jail"* and released the apostles (Acts 5:19). Later, when Peter was heavily guarded and chained, an angel appeared in response to the prayers of the church and led him to freedom (Acts 12:6–11).

► **Angels are agents in answering prayers**

In heaven an angel stands at the altar with incense to offer *"the prayers of all of the saints"* which go up before God from the angel's hand (Revelation 8:3, 4). And in the story Jesus told about Lazarus, it would seem that angels carry us into God's presence when we die (Luke 16:22).

If we are to do spiritual warfare, we need to pray for the help of God's holy angels!

9

The fight of faith

When the children of Israel were in slavery in Egypt, God supernaturally delivered them and brought them to the threshold of the promised land. At this point God spoke to their leader, Joshua, and said:

> *Get ready to cross the Jordan River into the land I am about to give to them – to the Israelites. I will give you every place where you set your foot, as I promised Moses.*
>
> (Joshua 1:2, 3)

Israel had to fight for the promised land. Although God had already provided it, there was something they still had to do in order to take possession of it. In dependence on God and in obedience to his instructions they had to get involved in warfare and seize what was promised.

As a result, most of the book of Joshua describes the various battles that they fought.

> *He captured all their kings and struck them down, putting them to death. Joshua waged war against all these kings for a long time. Except for the Hivites living in Gibeon, not one city made a treaty of peace with the Israelites, who took them all in battle ... So Joshua took the entire land, just as the Lord had directed Moses, and he gave it as an inheritance to Israel ... Then the land had rest from war.*
>
> (Joshua 11:17–19, 23)

Christians too have to fight for the inheritance promised to them. When Jesus died on the cross, he opened up to us all the blessings and promises of God.

> *For no matter how many promises God has made, they are "Yes" in Christ. And so through him the "Amen" is spoken by us to the glory of God.*   (2 Corinthians 1:20)

This abundant life only becomes ours, however, as we claim God's promises in faith. We speak *"Amen"* to his provision, to take hold of it.

If the enemy could have prevented the children of Israel from taking the entire land, he would have done so. If the devil can rob us of our rightful inheritance and deprive us of living in God's full provision, he will. Yet it is totally unacceptable for us as Christians to settle for less than abundant life. Jesus said,

> *"The thief comes only to steal and kill and destroy; I have come that they may have life, and have it to the full."*
> (John 10:10)

It seems as though the Lord has voted in our favor, the devil has voted against us, and we have to make the casting vote. For example, God wants us to experience the gifts of the Holy Spirit, while Satan is bent on us never knowing these manifestations of the power of God. Whether we ever receive them or not, depends on us. Exercising our faith is part of spiritual warfare.

After warning against wrong practices, Paul charged Timothy:

> *But you, man of God, flee from all this, and pursue right-eousness, godliness, faith, love, endurance and gentleness. Fight the good fight of the faith. Take hold of the eternal life to which you were called when you made your good confession in the presence of many witnesses.*   (1 Timothy 6:11–12)

We need to flee, follow and fight! Paul told Timothy to run

away from conceited behavior, an unhealthy interest in controversy and quarrels, envy, strife, malicious talk, evil suspicions, corruption and the love of money. He told him to follow after righteousness, godliness, faith, love, endurance and gentleness. Finally, Paul urged Timothy to fight the good fight of faith, to take hold of eternal life.

Fleeing and following produce character and the fruit of the Spirit. But we need to fight in faith to receive the promises of the kingdom. The writer of Hebrews said of the Old Testament heroes:

> ...*who through faith conquered kingdoms, administered justice, and gained what was promised; who shut the mouths of lions, quenched the fury of the flames, and escaped the edge of the sword; whose weakness was turned to strength; and who became powerful in battle and routed foreign enemies. Women received back their dead, raised to life again. Others were tortured and refused to be released, so that they might gain a better resurrection.* (Hebrews 11:33–35)

It takes the fight of faith to confront evil spirits and cast them out. It takes the fight of faith to secure healing, break the power of bad habits, or remove bondages.

It's time we fought the good fight of faith! Start fighting and keep on fighting. Fight with a determination to settle for nothing less than victory.

Paul told Timothy to *"take hold of the eternal life to which you were called."* We know that Timothy was a believer and had therefore already received the gift of eternal life. Yet eternal life is not only endless length of life, it refers to the quality of life. Eternal life is God's life in us, which should produce a harvest of blessing.

God's eternal life in us is surely more powerful than any sickness that the devil can put on our bodies. If we through the fight of faith lay hold of that eternal life, it will bring forth healing and health in us.

Imagine that you are holding a beautiful pearl in your hands, hugging it close to your chest. You know that this pearl has the power to heal you and bring blessing and prosperity. Yet imagine that someone is trying to steal this gem from you. The thief is weaker than you, but he is persistent.

You fight, and the thief retreats. After a while, the thief attacks again, and he keeps at this for a long time. Finally, imagine that you decide that things have gone too far, and you turn on the thief with all the strength you possess. The thief finally leaves you. You then walk away from the fight, cherishing the precious pearl which can now bring all the health and prosperity you need.

The eternal life of God is a treasure in every Christian. We need to hold it near and dear! When Satan tries to steal it from us, we need to fight him off until he leaves again. This will result in the fullness of salvation: deliverance, safety, preservation, healing and soundness. All these blessings were part of what Jesus accomplished for us on the cross.

The whole promised land became Israel's as the Israelites progressively fought for it. Our full inheritance in Christ will become ours in actual experience as we enter into spiritual warfare, fighting for what is rightfully ours.

Towards the end of his life, the apostle Paul wrote:

> *But you, keep your head in all situations, endure hardship, do the work of an evangelist, discharge all the duties of your ministry. For I am already being poured out like a drink offering, and the time has come for my departure. I have fought the good fight, I have finished the race, I have kept the faith. Now there is in store for me the crown of righteousness, which the Lord, the righteous Judge, will award to me on that day – and not only to me, but also to all who have longed for his appearing.* (2 Timothy 4:6–8)

For Paul, the fight was at times exceedingly difficult, even cruel. He worked hard, bore imprisonment and beatings, was shipwrecked, and faced the perils of robbers and false brethren. Satan is a wicked, merciless opponent. Yet despite the hardships Paul endured (read 2 Corinthians 11:23–28), he never backed down. Fighting the good fight, he emerged on the other side victorious and glorious – and few people have made such a mark for God in the world.

Paul wrote this encouragement to Timothy:

> *Timothy, my son, I give you this instruction in keeping with the prophecies once made about you, so that by following them you may fight the good fight, holding on to faith and a good conscience. Some have rejected these and so have ship-wrecked their faith.* (1 Timothy 1:18–19)

Paul indicated that prophetic words are fulfilled as we choose to walk in the purposes of God and fight the good fight of faith. This was true of Daniel, who understood Jeremiah's prophecy about the return to Jerusalem after seventy years. He set his face to seek God, bringing about spiritual warfare and ultimate victory (Daniel 9:2; 10:10–14).

We cannot be complacent about prophetic words that we have received for ourselves, our churches, or our nations. It is imperative that we exercise faith and keep a good conscience, so that the devil has no grounds for condemnation. Let's continue as faithful soldiers of the Lord Jesus Christ!

10

The armor of God

To constantly experience the victory of faith, we need to be dressed in the armor of God. Let's look at the famous passage in Ephesians chapter 6:10–18:

Finally, be strong in the Lord and in his mighty power.
(Ephesians 6:10)

This verse clearly states that the Lord's strength, power and might are available to all those who are part of the family of God. The statement *"be strong"* literally means, "be empowered."

How does this become a practical reality? Isaiah 40:31 has the answer. It says,

Those who hope in the LORD
will renew their strength.
They will soar on wings like eagles;
they will run and not grow weary,
they will walk and not be faint.

One paraphrase reads, "they shall switch over onto divine strength." As we put our hope in God, we receive his strength in place of our own.

Put on the full armor of God so that you can take your stand against the devil's schemes. (Ephesians 6:11)

Protected by God's armor, we are able to face all the schemes (literally, "methods") of the devil and still remain standing. We do not have to give way, and the devil need not get us down!

> *For our struggle is not against flesh and blood, but against the rulers, against the authorities, against the powers of this dark world and against the spiritual forces of evil in the heavenly realms.*   (Ephesians 6:12)

This is not a battle in physical terms, with worldly weapons. Our warfare is against invisible wicked forces in positions of authority. Even if we are physically weak, we can be spiritually strong.

> *Therefore put on the full armor of God, so that when the day of evil comes, you may be able to stand your ground, and after you have done everything, to stand.*   (Ephesians 6:13)

Because we fight a spiritual war, we must have spiritual protection. This armor enables us to stand our ground – the same Greek word translated "resist" in James 4:7: *"Resist the devil, and he will flee from you."*

Notice that wearing the armor of God does not mean that the devil will leave us alone. He will still attack us, but we have at our disposal all that we need to withstand the assaults. We must speak out and refuse the enemy access to any area that he is trying to oppress us in.

There is a battle, but it has been won. Each confrontation will eventually end: *"after you have done everything."* Then you can remain standing – in victory!

> *Stand firm, then, with the belt of truth buckled round your waist...*   (Ephesians 6:14a)

It is truth that helps us to stand firm. When he was tempted in the wilderness, Jesus resisted the enemy again and again with the truth of God: *"It is written..."* (Matthew 4:1–11).

Unless we know the truth, we will not be able to use it to stand firm against the enemy. The pattern is to hear (or read) the word, receive it with meekness, bind it around us, and then use it.

Truth is not only a matter of intellectual Bible knowledge. God's word must be in us, controlling our actions and attitudes, and affecting our entire lifestyle. We can't just know it cognitively – we must live it.

> *... with the breastplate of righteousness in place*
> (Ephesians 6:14b)

It is righteousness that protects our hearts. God has ascribed to believers the righteousness of Christ (2 Corinthians 5:21) because Jesus took our sin on the cross. With the breastplate of his righteousness in place, we are able to accept that *"there is now no condemnation for those who are in Christ Jesus"* (Romans 8:1). Freed from condemnation, we can have confidence in our personal prayers and in our ministry to others.

> *and with your feet fitted with the readiness that comes from the gospel of peace.*
> (Ephesians 6:15)

A look at the book of Acts will show that many angelic encounters took place, and gifts of the Holy Spirit were released, as the apostles went out soul-winning. God blesses us as we go out with the good news, protecting us and equipping us. We must be ready to take every opportunity to share the gospel of Jesus with others.

> *In addition to all this, take up the shield of faith, with which you can extinguish all the flaming arrows of the evil one.*
> (Ephesians 6:16)

The enemy can assault us with accusations and lies, capable of doing great damage. Yet with the shield of faith we can "quench the fiery darts" and nullify their power.

> *Take the helmet of salvation and the sword of the Spirit,*
> *which is the word of God.*   (Ephesians 6:17)

The salvation of Christ protects our minds, which is vital. Jesus said that the first and greatest commandment is *"Love the Lord your God with all your heart and with all your soul and with all your mind"* (Matthew 22:37). We can only fully do this as our minds are whole and sound.

Salvation is the great inclusive word of the gospel, covering forgiveness, deliverance, preservation, and healing of mind, body and spirit. It covers past, present and future. Through the sacrificial death of Jesus, we have been saved from the penalty of sin, we are presently being saved from the habits of sin, and ultimately we will be saved completely from all of sin's dominion.

The sword of the Spirit wields God's word to discern and destroy strongholds. Here the Christian is still advancing and on the offensive!

> *And pray in the Spirit on all occasions with all kinds of*
> *prayers and requests. With this in mind, be alert and always*
> *keep on praying for all the saints.*   (Ephesians 6:18)

An alert and active prayer life is vital in spiritual warfare. As we ask God for provision and listen to him, we are prepared for every eventuality and can "cover" our fellow believers when the battle gets intense.

11

God always comes through

We have seen that although the Christian life involves warfare, we have the overwhelming support of our God. God is a winner! He has never lost a battle and he never will.

If God is for us, who can be against us?   (Romans 8:31)

As long as we are walking in integrity before God, we will share his victory. If we rebel against him, however, we will be taken captive by the enemy.

The writer to the Hebrews said:

Remember those earlier days after you had received the light, when you stood your ground in a great contest in the face of suffering. Sometimes you were publicly exposed to insult and persecution; at other times you stood side by side with those who were so treated.   (Hebrews 10:32–33)

Coming into the light – receiving the revelation of Christ – brings us immediately into a war zone. It can involve suffering and exposure to insult and persecution, or standing by those who are suffering in this way. So often the enemy heaps pressure on us in an attempt to put out the light of God. Yet,

Do not throw away your confidence; it will be richly rewarded.
You need to persevere so that when you have done the will of
God, you will receive what he has promised.

(Hebrews 10:35–36)

We should not be surprised by problems and opposition or allow them to cause us to lose heart. If we bear in mind the great rewards of faith, each obstacle should be considered a stepping stone to further victory.

Perseverance doesn't just mean to grit our teeth and bear whatever comes our way. We must be continually open to the Spirit of God, listening to his voice. Sometimes in so doing we become aware of blockages or sin that need to be put right – things that otherwise give the devil a legal right to attack us. Only as we do the will of God can we expect release and the fulfillment of God's promises.

The writer to the Hebrews speaks of the return of Christ as judge and ruler on the earth. Those who shrink back are in danger of losing their eternal well-being. But those who have persevered in their faith will be saved in the Day of Judgment.

For in just a very little while,

   "He who is coming will come and will not delay.
    But my righteous one will live by faith.
   And I take no pleasure in the one who shrinks back."

But we are not of those who shrink back and are destroyed,
but of those who believe and are saved.

(Hebrews 10:37–39)

God always comes through, and he's never late!

12

Rebuking the devil

When we are facing the enemy, we dare to use the authority delegated to us by Jesus. We do this by speaking with our mouths. Therefore we can say something like this:

Lord Jesus, I acknowledge that you are my God. I willingly submit myself to your lordship over my life. Rule in my life, Lord Jesus.

And now, Satan and every evil spirit that is attacking me [you may wish to name a specific spirit], I resist you in the name of the Lord Jesus Christ. I refuse you any access to my life, my body, my family, my finances, my mind and my possessions. All that I have and am belongs to Jesus, the Son of the living God.

Satan, I break any hold you have on me. I have been washed in the blood of Jesus and so I am able to overcome you. I declare that you have no authority or right over me. Jesus lives in me and greater is he that is in me than is in the world.

Satan, I cast you out of my life. I break any influence you may have had over me and declare you to be the loser. You are totally defeated by the Lord Jesus Christ.

Satan, I bring the sword of the Spirit to bear against you. Jesus said,

"I have given you authority to trample on snakes and scorpions and to overcome all the power of the enemy; nothing will harm you." (Luke 10:19)

I believe that:

> *The weapons we fight with are not the weapons of the world. On the contrary, they have divine power to demolish strongholds.*   (2 Corinthians 10:4)

It is written:

> *Thanks be to God, who always leads us in triumphal procession in Christ.*   (2 Corinthians 2:14)

In the light of the word of God, I declare Satan to be defeated. Victory is mine in and through my King.

I worship you, Jesus, my Savior. Hallelujah!

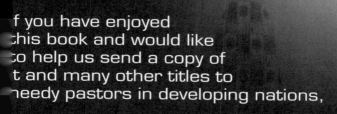

If you have enjoyed
this book and would like
to help us send a copy of
it and many other titles to
needy pastors in developing nations,

please write for further information,
or send your gift to:

Sovereign World Trust
PO Box 777
Tonbridge
Kent TN11 0ZS
United Kingdom

www.sovereignworldtrust.com